I CAN'T HANDLE
ALL THESE TRIALS

Joel James

Consulting Editor: Dr. Paul Tautges

Help! I Can't Handle All These Trials

© 2014 by Joel James

ISBN
Paper: 978-1-63342-066-3
ePub: ISBN 978-1-63342-067-0
Mobi: ISBN 978-1-63342-068-7

Published by **Shepherd Press**
P.O. Box 24
Wapwallopen, PA 18660

www.shepherdpress.com

All Scripture quotations, unless stated otherwise, are from the New American Standard Bible (NASB). Copyright © 1995 by The Lockman Foundation.

Designed by **documen**

CONTENTS

INTRODUCTION

This minibook grew out of a series of sermons that I preached at my church in 2002. In the previous months, our small church had faced death, brain tumors, cancer, child molestation, assault, family break-ups, financial collapse, and a host of lesser calamities.

In the course of a few weeks I counseled a woman who had seen her husband shot to death before her eyes, another who had contracted AIDS, a rape victim, and a friend who was in the midst of an ugly church split. At the same time, my wife was caught in the grip of an illness that left her often unable to get out of bed and left the doctors groping for solutions. I didn't feel like Job, but I did feel like Job's pastor.

In the face of all that, our church asked the same questions you ask when you face calamity: *Who is in control? Why did this happen? How should we respond?* As sailors seek shelter in a hurricane, so we turned to the Word of God and dropped anchor in the book of Job. For us, its lessons were the difference between faith and doubt, between hope and despair.

In the book of Job, we met a God so great, so wise, and so loving that we didn't have to understand why so many bad things were happening. With God leading us, we were content to walk by faith, not sight. I pray that through this minibook you'll learn the same lessons in fear-of-the-Lord faith that we did.

1

Who Is In Control?

I once read an interview with a woman whose home had been reduced to splinters by a tornado. Surveying the carnage, she told the reporter, "God wasn't in this. God didn't want this to happen." Is that true? Is God swept along in the flow of catastrophes such as tornadoes, unable to intervene? Are the tragic events of our lives—disasters, disease, and death—out of God's control? Those are important questions to answer biblically when you're caught up in the whirling winds of a calamity.

Many Christians believe that Satan is in control of calamity. In their view, Satan is almost equal to God in power—certainly he excels God in trickery. As you go through life, you always have to be looking over your shoulder, never sure when God might have his back turned, allowing Satan to run you down with some disaster God didn't anticipate.

Other people believe that *you* are in control of calamity, making yourself sick or causing a bad

month for your business by speaking or thinking
negative thoughts. In their view, if you think
positively enough and have faith enough, nothing
bad will happen to you.

Who is in control: Satan, you, or God? The
first two chapters of Job provide a definitive,
reassuring, biblical answer. When a tornado
flattens your home, a disease your health, or a
death your family—when everything seems out of
control—*God* is in control.

Meet Job

> There was a man in the land of Uz
> whose name was Job; and that man was
> blameless, upright, fearing God and
> turning away from evil.
>
> (Job 1:1)

Job was a real man who lived in Uz (an area of
northern Arabia) during the patriarchal era—
the time after the tower of Babel in Genesis 11,
but before God gave the Ten Commandments
in Exodus 20. Job was the epitome of what God
wanted an Old Testament man to be. He was
"blameless," morally complete—there were no
stains, spots, or blemishes on the garment of his

holiness. He was "upright"—straight as an arrow in all his ways. He was a fearer of God; he approached life with a humble, awed devotion to God. And Job habitually turned away from evil. Trying to get Job to do evil was like trying to push together the negative poles of two magnets—when it came to evil, Job always swerved away to the right or to the left. In short, Job was a bright trophy on God's mantelpiece of grace.

Besides his impeccable character, Job had also been blessed by God in other ways. With ten children, including seven sons to carry on the family name, and a livestock portfolio second to none, it's small wonder that the Bible calls Job the greatest man in all the East (v. 1:2–5).

Satan, the Accuser

> There was a day when the sons of God
> came to present themselves before the
> LORD, and Satan also came among them.
>
> (v. 1:6)

Among the angelic beings reporting to God was one called *Hasatan*, literally "the Adversary" or "the Accuser" in Hebrew. Later texts, such as Revelation 12:9, identify this being as the leader of the fallen angels, the devil, Satan, the same fallen angel who deceived Adam and Eve in the Garden of Eden. In Job 1, that lying, murderous Accuser had come for his regularly scheduled report to God.

> The LORD said to Satan, "Have you considered My servant Job? For there is no one like him on the earth, a blameless and upright man, fearing God and turning away from evil." Then Satan answered the LORD, "Does Job fear God for nothing? Have You not made a hedge about him and his house and all that he has, on every side? You have blessed the work of his hands, and his possessions have increased in the land. But put forth Your hand now and touch all that he has; he will surely curse You to Your face."
>
> (v. 1:8–11)

When God lionized Job, the Accuser immediately went on the attack. "Sure, I know all about Job. Why shouldn't he serve you? You give him everything he wants. But let me tell you a secret about Job that you don't know, God. Job is only in it for the blessings. Job doesn't love you; he loves what you give him. Take away his toys, and you'll see the real Job. Job likes sugar and bubbles, but when you stop giving him what he wants, he'll toss you aside like an empty soda can."

Satan was angry because God had thwarted his evil schemes by making "a hedge about [Job]" (v. 10). It was a hedge too high for Satan to climb over, too thick for him to cut his way through. In fact, Satan acknowledged that only one hand could cause calamity in Job's life: "But put forth *Your hand* now and touch all that he has; he will surely curse You to Your face" (v. 1:11, emphasis added).

Who is in control of calamity? By his own admission, Satan isn't. Without God's permission, Satan couldn't even make Job stub his toe. In verse 12, God gave permission to Satan to attack Job, but he also set strict limitations on Satan's assault:

> Then the LORD said to Satan, "Behold, all
> that he has is in your power, only do not
> put forth your hand on him."

Some Christians believe that God is taken by surprise or is helpless to intervene when Satan is working his evil schemes. However, they don't get that view from the Bible. Job 1 presents God as completely in charge of Job's calamity. First, God was the one who pointed Job out to Satan, initiating the whole affair. Second, Satan could not lay a finger on Job's possessions until he had God's permission to act. Third, God strictly limited Satan, forbidding him to attack Job's health at this point. Initiation, permission, and limitation—Satan was completely under God's control.

Further Evidence

Not just the book of Job, but the whole of Scripture proclaims the fact that God rather than Satan is in control of calamity. For example, Satan is not the source of physical handicaps, birth defects, or congenital diseases. God made that clear when Moses stubbornly resisted God's commission to lead his people because of his "heavy tongue."

> The LORD said to him, "Who has made man's mouth? Or who makes him mute or deaf, or seeing or blind? Is it not I, the LORD?"
>
> (Exodus 4:11)

Political corruption and violent crime are two calamities that many fear in the country of South

Africa where I live. When Jesus was unjustly arrested in the middle of the night and was legally murdered the next day, who was in control?

> This man, delivered over by the
> predetermined plan and foreknowledge
> of God, you nailed to a cross by the hands
> of godless men and put Him to death.
> (Acts 2:23)

Reflecting on the apparently out-of-control events of Jesus's arrest and crucifixion, Peter knew who had been in control. The indifferent, corrupt Roman authorities? The jealous, vengeful religious leaders? The ignorant execution squad? No. God and his predetermined plan.

Human words—positive or negative confession—also do not magically control good and bad. Jeremiah wrote,

> Who is there who speaks and it comes to
> pass, unless the Lord has commanded it?
> Is it not from the mouth of the Most High
> that both good and ill go forth?
> (Lamentations 3:37–38)

Solomon said it this way in Ecclesiastes 7:14:

> In the day of prosperity be happy, but in
> the day of adversity consider—God has
> made the one as well as the other.

Neither Satan nor positive or negative con-
fessions control calamity. God does. That is
exactly what we find in Job. Until God gave his
permission, Satan could touch neither Job nor his
possessions. In fact, although we know Satan had
a personal hand in Job's calamities, Job was never
encouraged to handle his situation by binding
Satan, casting off curses, speaking positive con-
fessions, or by employing any of the other occult-
like techniques so popular in some parts of the
church today. The book of Job ends with Job back
on track. What was the secret? He focused on
God; Satan and demons are not even mentioned.

A Day of Destruction

As we take up the narrative of Job 1 again, we
find that in a day of frenzied destruction Satan
engineered four separate disasters designed to ruin
Job (v. 1:13–19). All Job's oxen and donkeys were
stolen and his servants slaughtered. All his sheep
were destroyed by lightning and the shepherds
incinerated. All his camels were kidnapped and

their guardians massacred. But by far the most devastating calamity on that day of holocausts was the death of Job's children, crushed by a cascade of bricks as a tornado leveled the eldest son's house.

Job's response to his ruin was a fear-of-the-Lord response:

> Then Job arose and tore his robe and
> shaved his head, and he fell to the ground
> and worshipped.
>
> (v. 1:20)

Tearing the robe, shaving the head, and falling to the ground were common expressions of grief in Job's culture. Worshiping was not. But Job was an uncommon man.

> "Naked I came from my mother's womb,
> and naked I shall return there. The
> LORD gave and the LORD has taken
> away. Blessed be the name of the LORD."
> Through all this Job did not sin nor did
> he blame God.
>
> (v. 1:21–22)

Job acknowledged that all he had received in life had been God's gift—none of it was deserved. And what God gave, God had the right to take away. The end of verse 22 literally reads, "Job did not ascribe folly to God." In other words, Job did not accuse God of making a mistake when he took the life of his children and his employees and left Job in financial ruin.

If At First You Don't Succeed …

Job had not folded under pressure as Satan had predicted. However, the Accuser was quick to find an explanation: God had not touched that which was most dear to Job, his own precious skin. "Strike his health, God," squealed Satan, "and Job will turn on you faster than a striking cobra."

> Put forth Your hand now, and touch his bone and his flesh; he will curse You to Your face.
>
> (v. 2:5)

Notice again Satan's acknowledgment that God was in control. He begged God, "Put forth *Your* hand …" Satan may do the actual deed, but he knows full well who is in charge.

So the LORD said to Satan, "Behold, he is

in your power, only spare his life."

(v. 2:6)

Having sought and obtained permission (but again with a critical limitation), Satan launched his second attack, striking Job with boils. Job was covered from head to foot with agonizing, swollen, burning, oozing sores. And the treatment was no party either:

And he took a potsherd to scrape himself
while he was sitting among the ashes.

(v. 2:8)

The "ashes" referred to the place where the household refuse was burned. Job's hospital bed was a garbage heap.

His wife encouraged him to give up the battle and die, but Job refused to adopt an attitude of bitter resentment:

"Shall we indeed accept good from God
and not accept adversity?" In all this Job
did not sin with his lips.

(v. 2:10)

Who Is In Control of Calamity?

The opening two chapters of Job answer the question "Who is in control of calamity?" with unmistakable clarity. Job, Satan, and God all confirmed that *God* is in control. In short, God controlled the origin, timing, nature, and extent of Job's calamities.

When life feels out of control like an airplane in a flat spin, it's comforting to know that God's hand is on the stick and that his feet are on the rudder pedals. To handle your calamity in a trusting, God-honoring way, you must be convinced that God is in control and that he knows how to land the plane.

But that leads to a second question. If God is in control, why did God allow Satan to pillage Job's possessions, pulverize his family, and punch Job's health in the nose? If God is in control, why does he allow bad things to happen at all? To answer that question, we need to consider the next section of Job.

2

Why Did This Happen?

My wife is fond of saying, "There are no accidents in God's program," because our calamities are actually God's carefully crafted plan. However, that assures us only momentarily: "What a relief that God is in control ... [pause] ... But if God is in control, *why* did he allow this painful thing to happen?" There are at least five reasons God brings calamity into the lives of his people. One of those takes center stage in the book of Job, so let's consider it first.

Is This God's Judgment?

The *first reason* God causes calamity is to *discipline someone for specific sin*. But be careful! It was their misapplication of this principle that led Job's friends off track. Many make the same mistake today; therefore, let's carefully consider this point.

At first, Job didn't demand answers from God when God brought disaster on him (v. 1:22; 2:10).

However, over time Job's trust in God was devoured by a locust swarm of demanding "Why?" questions.

> Why did I not die at birth? Come forth
> from the womb and expire?
>
> (v. 3:11)

> Why is light given to him who suffers?
> (v. 3:20a)

> Why then have You brought me out of
> the womb? ... [Why will] He not let my
> few days alone? Withdraw from me that I
> may have a little cheer.
>
> (v. 10:18, 20)

> Have I sinned? What have I done to You,
> O watcher of men? Why have you set me
> as Your target?
>
> (v. 7:20)

When Job asked, "Why has this happened?" the theologians in Job's world were, as we shall see presently, happy to supply him with what they believed was the right answer: "God is disciplining you for your sin."

Does God discipline people with calamity for specific sins they have committed? Yes ... sometimes. King David destroyed his life in exchange for a few minutes of pleasure with Bathsheba. But his life wasn't the only one that David destroyed. God brought calamity—the death of their infant son—on David and Bathsheba as judgment for their adultery (2 Samuel 12:15, 18). King Uzziah of Judah was struck with leprosy when he violated God's law by trying to offer a sacrifice in the temple, something only priests from the tribe of Levi were allowed to do (2 Chronicles 26:16–19). And it wasn't only royalty that incurred this kind of judgment. Gehazi was just a servant, but he was also struck by God with leprosy when he lied to Elisha about taking money from Naaman (2 Kings 5:20–27).

Sometimes God does cause calamity in order to discipline people for specific sins. Tragically, Job's friends misapplied that principle to Job, with devastating effect—as we shall now see.

The Visit

When word of Job's catastrophes spread, there was great concern among Job's acquaintances. Three of them, Eliphaz, Bildad, and Zophar—

wisdom experts like Job himself—determined that they would visit Job in an attempt to comfort him. When they arrived at Job's house, they were shocked by what they found.

> When they lifted up their eyes at a
> distance and did not recognize him, they
> raised their voices and wept. And each of
> them tore his robe and they threw dust
> over their heads toward the sky. Then
> they sat down on the ground with him for
> seven days and seven nights with no one
> speaking a word to him, for they saw that
> his pain was very great.
>
> (v. 2:12–13)

Enthroned on ashes and covered with maggots, filth, scabs, and oozing sores, Job was unrecognizable to his friends. His complaint, "So am I allotted months of vanity" (v. 7:3), suggests that he had been in this pitiful state for several months before they arrived. In verse 7:14 Job spoke of hallucinations, a common result of significant sleep loss. He had no hope and would have given anything for a restful night's sleep.

> When I lie down I say, "When shall I

> arise?" But the night continues, and I am
> continually tossing until dawn. My flesh
> is clothed with worms and a crust of dirt,
> my skin hardens and runs ... My days ...
> come to an end without hope.
>
> (v. 7:4–6)

Observing Job's misery, his friends broke their silence. Unanimously accepting that God was in control, they took it upon themselves to explain why God had ruined Job.

As we consider this, you must grasp a significant point: Job's friends were both right and wrong at the same time. They were correct in saying that God does use calamity to discipline specific sin. Their mistake, however, was assuming that that is the *only* reason God brings calamity, and therefore, that it must be true in Job's case.

Eliphaz was the first to speak. His opening salvo is a summary of everything he and his companions would say in the next twenty chapters.

> Remember now, who ever perished being
> innocent? Or where were the upright
> destroyed? According to what I have seen,
> those who plow iniquity and those who
> sow trouble harvest it. By the breath of

God they perish and by the blast of His
anger they come to an end.

(v. 4:7–9)

Eliphaz had a simple theology of calamity. If you live rightly, God blesses you. If you live badly, God drops a bomb on you. Job had obviously taken a direct hit from the biggest bomb in God's arsenal; therefore, he must have been living badly.

Convinced that they were right, Eliphaz and his friends tightened their philosophical fingers around Job's throat with clear references to his agonizing physical condition.

» Eliphaz: "Affliction does not come from the dust ... The wicked man writhes in pain all his days" (v. 5:6; 15:20).

» Bildad: "Indeed, the light of the wicked goes out ... His skin is devoured by disease" (v. 18:5, 13).

» Zophar: "If iniquity is in your hand, put it far away ... then, indeed, you could lift up your face without moral defect" (v. 11:14–15).

The relentless accusations of Job's friends had the same effect on Job that accusations of a lack of faith or hidden sin have on sick or hurting Christians today. They frustrated and dispirited him.

> You smear with lies; you are all worthless
> physicians. O that you would be
> completely silent, and that it would
> become your wisdom!
>
> (v. 13:4–5)

> My spirit is broken, my days are
> extinguished, the grave is ready for me.
> Surely mockers are with me, and my eye
> gazes on their provocation.
>
> (v. 17:1–2)

Job's calamities were devastating enough without his friends heaping insult on agony. Instead of untrue accusations, Job longed for comfort from them:

> For the despairing man there should be
> kindness from his friend; so that he does
> not forsake the fear of the Almighty.
>
> (v. 6:14)

Job's resistance to their accusations infuriated his friends; therefore, Eliphaz eventually stripped off the gloves and let Job have it right on the chin.

> *Is it because of your reverence that*
> *He reproves you, that He enters into*
> *judgment against you? Is not your*
> *wickedness great?*
>
> (v. 22:4–5a)

"Job, do you think God has done all this to you because you are such a great guy? Because you are so godly? That's ridiculous, Job!" Actually, it wasn't ridiculous at all. How had God described Job in chapters 1 and 2? "There is no one like him on the earth, a blameless and upright man, fearing God and turning away from evil" (v. 1:8; 2:3). Derek Kidner has rightly said of Job, "It was his very innocence that exposed him to the ordeal."[1]

Unfortunately, the reductionistic view of calamity held by Job's friends is still with us. You know the scenario. A Christian is in the hospital with a devastating illness such as cancer, and some well-meaning acquaintances show up and say, "If you had enough faith, you would be healed" or "You must have secret sin in your life. That's why this is happening to you."

To face calamity, you must embrace this lesson

---

1 Derek Kidner, *The Wisdom of Proverbs, Job and Ecclesiastes* (Downers Grove, IL: InterVarsity Press, 1985), 57.

from the book of Job: a catastrophe in health, finances, or family doesn't necessarily mean that God is angry at you. Occasionally God does use calamity to discipline a specific sin; however, Job's terrible losses and ravaged body had nothing to do with a lack of faith or hidden iniquity. In fact, at the end of Job's book God was righteously angry at Eliphaz, Bildad, and Zophar for insisting that Job's calamities must have been the result of his secret sin (v. 42:7).

Our Lord Jesus Christ was also no friend of Eliphaz's criminally simplistic, "You must have been bad" view of calamity, something his disciples learned in John 9.

> *As He passed by, He saw a man blind from birth. And His disciples asked Him, "Rabbi, who sinned, this man or his parents, that he would be born blind?"*
> (John 9:1–2)

The disciples had exactly the same theology of sickness as Eliphaz, Bildad, and Zophar. Jesus was quick to correct it:

> *It was neither that this man sinned, nor his parents; but it was so that the works*

of God might be displayed in him.

(v. 9:3)

Many Christians today fall into the trap of Job's three friends, assuming that calamity comes for only one reason. As a result, they often unjustly accuse suffering people, stealing their hope that, in the midst of their tragedy, God still loves them. To steal that hope is a theft more cruel than any other. God's fury with Eliphaz, Bildad, and Zophar in Job 42:7 serves as a warning against it.

If there is no obvious cause-and-effect relationship between your calamity and a specific sin, you don't have to torture yourself trying to divine what the sin is for which God is disciplining you. Of course, if you are harboring sin you need to repent from, by all means do so! But don't fall into the trap of Job's friends, accusing others (or yourself) of being out of God's favor because they or you have experienced a tragedy. Cancer, crime, or car accidents aren't proof that God is angry at you.

"But," you ask, "if God isn't disciplining me for a specific sin, why did he allow this to happen?" Let's step aside from the book of Job for a moment to answer that question from the rest of Scripture.

Other Reasons God Brings Calamity

After disciplining a specific sin, a *second reason* God brings calamity is *because of human sin generally.* In Genesis 3, Adam pulled the keystone out of the arch of creation with his sin, and ever since, bricks have been falling on our heads. When Adam sinned, the whole universe was plunged into futility and enslaved to corruption (Romans 8:20–22). In our bodies that means pain and infections. In our work that means weeds, forms in triplicate, and software that self-destructs during an important sales presentation. In relationships it means parental distraction, teenage disruption, and messy divorces.

We can praise God that Jesus Christ has defeated the Curse and has accomplished its ultimate removal through his death on the cross. The book of Revelation describes heaven with these seven powerful words:

> There will no longer be any curse.
> (Revelation 22:3)

But in the meantime, we can be sure that one reason calamity comes is because of human sinfulness generally.

Under Construction

A *third reason* God brings calamity is *to mature believers in Jesus Christ* (if you have not yet put your faith in Christ for the forgiveness of sin, God is using your trial, not to *mature* you in Christ, but to *move* you toward Christ). As a believer in Jesus Christ, you can be sure that, whatever happens, God is causing it to bring his Christ-reflecting and Christ-exalting work in you one step closer to completion.

> *Consider it all joy, my brethren, when you encounter various trials, knowing that the testing of your faith produces endurance. And let endurance have its perfect result, so that you may be perfect and complete, lacking in nothing.*
>
> (James 1:2–4)

To make a sword requires *heating* and *beating*. In the same way, comfort, peace, and ease don't produce spiritually strong, flexible, sharp Christians. Only the heating and beating of God-given trials manufactures resilient, Christlike character—a blade strong enough and sharp enough to be truly useful in the hand of God.

God used my wife's illness (mentioned in the Introduction) that way in our family. No one likes to be bedridden, but my wife became more patient with sickness, and more accepting of the good and the bad from God. With Mom out of action, our kids learned to be better helpers around the house. Even Dad learned to do dishes with a cheerful heart. We all became sharper and stronger instruments in God's hands because of it.

Just as a weight lifter doesn't become stronger unless he exhausts his muscles moving chunks of iron, so spiritual progress comes only when God the Coach increases the intensity for us through painful trials. When he does so, the result is stronger faith, greater compassion, and enduring patience—firmer spiritual muscles in every way.

Faith on Parade

A *fourth reason* God brings calamity into the lives of believers is *to prove our faith*, both to ourselves and to others. How did God prove that Satan's accusations against Job were slanderous? God tested Job, and Job's endurance proved Satan to be wrong.

Peter told his readers that they had been embroiled in trials because the proof of their faith was more precious than gold. And when their faith eventually came through the crucible pure and strong, Peter said that their endurance would

> result in praise and glory and honor at the revelation of Jesus Christ.
>
> (1 Peter 1:6–7)

We had a woman in our church who had cancer twelve different times before she finally went to be with the Lord. It was hard in every way—physically, emotionally, and spiritually. But as we watched her resilient, God-given cheerfulness, we couldn't help but be encouraged. The proof of her faith in Christ spurred us to trust the Lord more ourselves.

Unanticipated Good

A *fifth reason* God brings calamity into the lives of his people is *to bring about unanticipated good*. The Bible is full of such surprises. The classic example? Joseph (Genesis 37–50). His brothers kidnapped him and sold him into slavery just as they might have auctioned off a cow or goat to the highest bidder. No doubt as the slave traders' camel caravan humped its way toward

Egypt (and at various awkward points after that) Joseph asked, "Why has God done this?" Answer: unexpected good.

Eventually God used Joseph's kidnapping, slavery, and unjust imprisonment to put him in a position to keep his family from starvation. Decades later, Joseph said to his brothers,

> As for you, you meant evil against me, but God meant it for good in order to bring about this present result, to preserve many people alive.
>
> (Genesis 50:20)

No one could have guessed it at the time, but *good* was God's plan for Joseph's calamities all along.

Ruth provides another example. Tragedy doesn't come much worse than having your father-in-law, brother-in-law, and husband die in rapid succession, leaving you and your mother-in-law impoverished and hopeless. How did God use that heartrending situation? Ruth went to a place she would never otherwise have gone to (Bethlehem), met a man she would never otherwise have met (Boaz), married him, and became the great-grandmother of King David and part of the Messiah's line. Unexpected good.

It's all over the Bible—apparently unsalvageable disasters are often the first step in God's plan for bringing good.

All this helps us see that calamity isn't arbitrary. God uses it for specific purposes: occasionally to discipline specific sin, but more often to make us dissatisfied enough with this sinful world to seek something (or Someone) better, to harden us in the furnace of troubles just as a blacksmith tempers a sword, to prove our faith, and to bring good that no one could have predicted.

Up to this point, we have discovered that God is in control and we have identified the biblical reasons why he causes calamity. But how should we respond when God stokes the forge, pumps the bellows, and swings the hammer, relentlessly shaping and sharpening the sword of our faith in Christ?

3

Why Job Stumbled

Job started so well. His faith was as invulnerable to Satan's onslaughts as a turtle snuggled up inside its shell is to the frantic pawings of a dog. Job tucked his head and feet inside his faith in God and said, "The Lord gives, the Lord takes away. Blessed be the name of the Lord." What went wrong? There are at least four reasons Job's trust in God took a tumble. First, he listened to bad counsel.

Avoid Bad Counsel

If you are going to handle your calamity in a wise, God-honoring manner, you must *ignore well-intentioned but unbiblical counsel.* If Job's counselors had been from the church in our era, they probably would have said, "Job, look at these terrible things that are happening to you. We have to break the generational curses that have power over your life. We have to cast out the demons of skin disease. You need to send 500 dollars to the faith-healer, I. M. Acharlatan, at Better-for-a-Buck Ministries."

People will say all kinds of crazy things to you when calamity strikes ("Don't worry, God didn't know this was going to happen." Really? Now I *am* worried!). Don't let their well-intended but unbiblical counsel trip you up spiritually and send you sprawling. To handle calamity, you must ignore unbiblical advice with a gentle smile and a thank you. People speak to you because they care; receive their counsel with a gracious attitude, but don't let their unbiblical advice throw you into a tailspin like Job did.

Time Keeps On Tickin'

A second reason Job went off the rails was that he let the termite of time gnaw at his faith. According to Job 7:3, Job's grief and the burning torment of his physical ailments had extended for months by the time his friends arrived. Job's suffering felt eternal; the sheer duration of it was wearing him down.

Like an eager marathon runner, Job bolted off the starting line of faith, but as the race of responding to his calamity stretched out mile after mile and day after day, Job's faith began to stumble and stagger. Time is a killer in trials. Like Job, we start with strong faith, but as we tick off days on the calendar, turn over the page to a new month, eventually buy a new calendar for next year, and then a new one for the year after that, we can easily despair. Time makes trials hard.

When I ran track in high school, although I was a distance runner, our coach occasionally made us do sprint workouts. Our deepest hatred was reserved for the workout in which he said, "Start sprinting as hard as you can, and don't stop until I blow the whistle." It was brutal. We never knew how long he was going to make us sprint. There was no finish line to cross. We just had to keep running, not knowing when the whistle would bring relief.

Some trials are like that. You don't know when things are going to get better; you just have to keep trusting God, unsure when he will blow the whistle so you can catch your breath. How can you keep time from weakening your faith?

Daily Reliance Upon Grace

Jesus addresses this issue when he says,

> *Do not worry about tomorrow; for tomorrow will care for itself. Each day has*

enough trouble of its own.

(Matthew 6:34)

His point is that God gives grace one day at a time—for today, not for tomorrow.

Blessed be the Lord, who daily bears our burden, the God who is our salvation.

(Psalm 68:19)

The LORD's lovingkindnesses indeed never cease, for His compassions never fail. They are new every morning; great is Your faithfulness.

(Lamentations 3:22–23)

God's grace is perfectly sufficient to tackle the challenges of the day he gives that grace. But his grace will always prove inadequate if you try to spread it across tomorrow's problems as well. It's like buttering bread—the dab of butter that's more than adequate to cover one slice gets a bit thin if you try to spread it over a whole loaf. In the same way, don't try to spread God's strength for today over tomorrow, next month, or next year. Planning ahead is fine; worrying ahead isn't.

Handle today with a joyful, dependent, God-trusting attitude. Tomorrow will have new troubles *and* new grace. But sometimes even a single day feels too long to face. What do you do then? Do the next right thing. That is Jesus's principle, honed to a needle's point. Sufficient is the trouble for the *minute*. Whatever the next right thing is—getting out of bed, cooking a meal, or going to work—do it, trusting God's grace.

The Expectations Trap

In chapter 29, Job listed his many accomplishments. For example:

» He was a respected civic leader: "When I went out to the gate of the city ... the old men arose and stood" (v. 29:7–8).

» He was adored by the poor and disadvantaged because of his philanthropy: "I was eyes to the blind and feet to the lame" (v. 29:15).

» In summary he declared, "My steps were bathed in butter, and the rock poured out for me streams of oil!" (v. 29:6).

Because of his success and his great kindness to others, Job had built up some *expectations*— things he believed God owed him because he had been good. In chapter 30, Job had this flash of insight into his confused and angry heart.

> When I expected good, then evil came;
> when I waited for light, then darkness
> came. I am seething within and cannot
> relax; days of affliction confront me.
>
> (v. 30:26–27)

Job had stepped directly into the expectations trap. Job expected good from God because he had been good, and when God didn't deliver, Job was left seething. It's an easy trap to fall into when calamity strikes. "All I wanted was a happy family, and now my daughter is divorced ... my son is rebelling ... my husband has left me. What did I do to deserve this?" The expectation? If I'm a good wife and mother, God owes me a happy family, as I define it.

A friend of mine whose child has Down Syndrome once shared with me that expectations are one of the greatest struggles faced by parents of handicapped children: "All I wanted was to watch my boy play sports, see him go to college, get married, and have a successful career. Now I have a son who will never pass grade two." Expectations can be a real problem when we face calamity. Job's summary is both pathetic and perfect: "When I expected good, then evil came" (v. 30:26).

The expectation that God owes me good if I have been good is dangerous because it leads to feelings of betrayal and anger at God. God, however, never promises endless good if we are a devoted mother, a patient father, a faithful taxpayer, or if we don't run with the wrong crowd at school. To handle calamity rightly, Christians must avoid Job's mistake of building up the expectation that "God owes me because I've tried to be good."

The Shield of Faith

Besides bad counsel, time, and expectations, there was one other thing that made Job stumble: *he lost his grip on the shield of faith*. In chapters 1–2, Job was solidly entrenched behind an impenetrable barrier of faith in God's wisdom—a perfect example of Paul's teaching about the shield of faith in Ephesians 6.

> Take up the full armor of God ... taking up the shield of faith with which you will be able to extinguish all the flaming arrows of the evil one.
>
> (Ephesians 6:13, 16)

The soldiers of the ancient world often carried large shields. When enemy archers fired a volley of arrows, they ducked behind those shields and let the arrows harmlessly ricochet off. In Job 1–2, Job had done just that. Satan had fired a barrage of fiery darts at him, but the shield of Job's faith had deflected them all. That's how faith works: no arrow of Satan—no matter how hot or deadly—can overwhelm simple, childlike faith: "I'll trust God whether I understand what he is doing or not."

In chapter 3, Job allowed the handle of the shield of faith to slip from his sweaty fingers. Rather than preoccupy himself with believing trust, Job allowed his thinking to be dominated by frustrated expectations and, later, by the disheartening, untrue accusations of his friends.

In the Gospels, the man cried, "I do believe; help my unbelief" (Mark 9:24). In calamity, we must voice a similar cry to Christ: "I believe; rescue me from my doubt, fear, anger, and unbelief." How do we go about hiding behind the shield of faith in calamity? Let's return to the story of Job to find the answer.

4

Fear-of-the-Lord Faith

As the shield of Job's faith slipped lower and lower, he did one of the most devastating things someone can do when facing calamity: Job asked the question "Why?" Asking "Why?" isn't a bad thing if we accept God's biblical answers. God brings calamity to mature us, to prove our faith, to bring unexpected good, and so on. However, very often (as was the case with Job) we are dissatisfied with God's biblical answers. We want (and believe we *deserve*) a specific explanation as to why our catastrophe has happened.

In the middle of calamity, people sometimes oscillate between desperate pleading with and open hostility toward God: "Why did *I* have to get cancer and not someone else? Why was *our* house broken into? Why did *my* mother die? I hate God for what he has done." When a calamity strikes, we become negotiators, offering God alternative (and in our minds, far better) plans: "Why wasn't it someone who doesn't like sports who was paralyzed? Why did I have to lose my job now, just when my wife has become pregnant with our first child?"

What those questions imply is, "God, you've made a mistake, and I want an opportunity to argue with you about it. You did this to the wrong person at the wrong time. Before you take this thing any further, I want to see your plan so I can make sure I approve of it."

Is a divine explanation as to why God allowed your crisis the key to handling calamity? Is an explanation regarding how your disaster fits into his overall plan the secret to a trusting response? You might think so, but the book of Job reveals how wrong you are. From chapter 3 on, Job begged, pleaded with, and railed against God. He threw himself at the door of heaven, pounding, kicking, and screaming, demanding answers. He pounded until his fists were bruised and bloody, and he shouted until his voice was hoarse. But in the end, Job's fury was silenced. His questions vanished. He stood with his hand over his mouth—as graphic a way of expressing "I have nothing to say" as I can imagine. Did God give Job a lengthy explanation of why he did what he did? Did God divulge the information that Job wanted? No.

As you read to the end of the book of Job, you find a startling thing. As far as we know, Job was never told about the heavenly dialogue between God and Satan in chapters 1–2. Furthermore, God didn't tell Job that his calamity would be reversed or that he would insert it in the Bible so that Job's story would encourage millions of believers for millennia to come.

The secret to Job's change of heart in chapters 40–42 was not *information*. It was a *Person*. At the end of the book, Job met a Person so great and so wise that all of Job's accusations, arguments, and questions melted away like an ice cube in the summer sun. In the end, Job found consolation, comfort, and satisfaction, not in an explanation, but in God. Or to say it another way, Job found consolation, comfort, and satisfaction in the fear of the Lord. But let's not just summarize the story. Let's observe Job's frustration, anger, and accusations, and then press past them to his restoration to a fear-of-the-Lord faith.

Thinking the Unthinkable

Tortured both in body and spirit, Job was so convinced that God had wrongfully assailed him that he demanded an opportunity to debate with God. The idea of a disputation or court case to prove his innocence first occurred to Job in chapter 9. Initially, the idea was to Job monstrous, unthinkable.

> *If one wished to dispute with [God], he*
> *could not answer Him once in a thousand*
> *times.*
>
> (v. 9:3)

"If I had a thousand opportunities to debate with God," sighed Job, "I couldn't beat him even once." Job was certain that God-All-Wise had blundered, but he couldn't contemplate arguing with *God*. However, by chapter 13, what had initially been unthinkable became Job's driving passion:

> *I would speak to the Almighty, and I*
> *desire to argue with God.*
>
> (v. 13:3)

So strong was Job's desire to extract an explanation from God that in chapter 23 Job begged for a hearing in God's courtroom.

> *Oh that I knew where I might find Him,*
> *that I might come to His seat! I would*
> *present my case before Him and fill my*
> *mouth with arguments.*
>
> (v. 23:3-4)

Given a chance to argue it out, Job believed that he could prove that God should not have brought his calamities on him. Job was certain that he could sift through God's plans and show God where he had overlooked a superior alternative to crushing Job and his family. When God was faced with the arguments he could muster, Job was sure that God would be forced to acknowledge his error and restore Job's fortunes.

In short, in the opening verses of chapter 23, Job issued a subpoena, calling God to court. In doing so, however, Job was in a terrible predicament. The only judge qualified to hear his case was the very God he was accusing. In fact, at one time or another in chapters 3–31, Job put God in every seat in the courtroom. Because of the false accusations of his obstinate friends, Job called God as a *witness* to his innocence. God was also the only one who could *judge* whether Job or his friends were correct. And now Job wanted to make God the *defendant*, facing Job's accusations of injustice and criminally bad management.

Having abandoned submissive faith, Job was spinning like a demagnetized compass needle. But in it all Job was certain that, if only he could speak to God face-to-face, he could convince him that the death of his children, the loss of his wealth, and the collapse of his health were all a gigantic mistake.

A New Voice

In chapter 32, a new voice entered the dialogue with Job. After endless wrangling, the debate between Job, Eliphaz, Bildad, and Zophar had ground to a standstill (v. 32:1). Job wouldn't admit to any gruesome, secret sin to explain what God had done, and they wouldn't accept Job's protest-ations of innocence. Enter Elihu.

Elihu's most significant contribution to the discussion was his emphasis that God was not responsible for explaining anything to Job.

> [Job,] you are not right in this, for God is
> greater than man. Why do you complain
> against Him that He does not give an
> account of all His doings?
>
> (v. 33:12–13)

Elihu also challenged Job's assertion that he knew better than God how to arrange his life. Elihu did this by directing Job's attention to the complexity and grandeur of the physical creation.

> Listen to this, O Job, stand and consider
> the wonders of God. Do you know how
> God establishes them, and makes the
> lightning of His cloud to shine? Do
> you know about the layers of the thick
> clouds? ... Can you, with Him, spread out
> the skies?
>
> (v. 37:14–16, 18)

This turn of argument—"How can you contend with the God who made the world?"—is vital. It is exactly the argument God used when he answered Job's summons.

God's Day in Court

In chapter 23, Job called God to court to answer accusations of injustice and mismanagement. In chapter 38, an astonishing thing happened: God showed up. In the visible manifestation of a great storm cloud and tornado, God answered Job's call to court.

Even more astounding than the fact that God came to speak with Job is what God said when he arrived. Job spent chapter after chapter pleading for, begging, and demanding answers from God. How many answers did God give Job when he arrived? None. That's right. Not one.

"Why didn't I die at birth? Why don't you leave me alone so I can have some peace? Why are you crushing me? Why? *Why? WHY?*" God did not answer one of Job's questions. Instead—this is a hard pill for our pride to swallow—God questioned Job's right to ask them.

> Then the LORD answered Job out of
> the whirlwind, and said, "Who is this
> that darkens counsel by words without
> knowledge?"
>
> (v. 38:1–2)

What is God's accusation against Job? Ignorance. Job was asking questions about things he couldn't understand. God's monologue in chapters 38–41 can be summed up by this question: "Job, do you really think you know better than I do how to arrange your life and the lives of those you love?"

Wisdom vs. Wisdom

At first reading, God's response to Job in chapters 38–41 seems strange, as if he were avoiding the real issue with an avalanche of irrelevant questions about snow, deer giving birth, and binding wild oxen. But God's questions are never irrelevant. How did those things relate to Job's accusation that God had mismanaged his life?

Job and his fellow Old Testament wisdom experts rightly considered God's creating and daily administration of the physical universe to be a profound testimony of God's matchless wisdom and organizational skill. For example, Proverbs 3:19 says,

> The LORD by wisdom founded the earth,
> by understanding He established the
> heavens.
>
> (see also Proverbs 8:22–30)

Therefore, although God's tour of the creation in Job 38–41 might seem strange to us, Job understood perfectly what God was doing: "Job, let's have a contest. You believe I have mismanaged your affairs; let's have a contest to see who has the greater wisdom, you or I. We'll keep it simple, Job. The physical universe will be our test case. If you can order it better than I can, then we'll talk about who gets to order your life."

And so, beginning in chapter 38, God gave Job a tour of creation. At every point, God's question

was, "Job, can you explain how this works? Do
you know how the bird flies? How the fish swims?
Where the lightning comes from? Do you know
when the animals should give birth? How to make
the sun rise and set? Where I keep the food for the
lions? Job, could you order the physical universe
for even *one day*?" With gently chiding questions,
God pointed out how laughable the idea of Job
ordering and running the universe was.

» "Where were you when I laid the foundation
  of the earth? Tell Me, if you have
  understanding, who set its measurements?
  ... On what were its bases sunk? Or who laid
  its cornerstone?" (v. 38:4–7). "Job, could you
  have designed, created, and assembled the
  universe from nothing—with no blueprint, no
  raw materials?"

» "I placed boundaries on [the sea], and set a
  bolt and doors, and I said, 'Thus far you shall
  come, but no farther; and here shall your
  proud waves stop' (v. 38:10–11). "Job, can you
  tell the sea where to stop? Would it listen to
  you if you did?"

» "Have you ever in your life commanded the
  morning, and caused the dawn to know its

place?" (v. 38:12). "Where is the way to the dwelling of light? And darkness, where is its place? ... Have you entered the storehouses of the snow, or have you seen the storehouses of the hail?" (v. 38:19, 22).

Job wasn't saying much at this point. Clearly his answer was, "No, God, I don't know how to make the sun rise and set, where you keep the rain and snow, or which drawer you keep the light in." Job was like the average husband in the kitchen: he didn't have a clue where things were or how to use them. Putting Job in charge of the universe for a day would be like putting a two-year-old in the cockpit of a Boeing 747 and saying, "Land it."

> Then the LORD said to Job, "Will the
> faultfinder contend with the Almighty?
> Let him who reproves God answer
> it." Then Job answered the LORD and
> said, "Behold, I am insignificant; what
> can I reply to You? I lay my hand on
> my mouth."
>
> (v. 40:1–4)

Having given Job a tour of creation, God finished proving his wisdom and majesty by taking

Job to the zoo in the rest of chapters 40–41. There he showed Job the two greatest animals in his creation: Behemoth and Leviathan. With bones like tubes of bronze, tails that swung back and forth like trees bending in a gale, gigantic stomachs, necks that allowed them to feed on water plants even when a river was at flood stage, and armor-plating (v. 40:15–23; 41:13), these animals sound like what we call dinosaurs—the kind of creature that God would show Job as "first" in his creation (v. 40:19).

By the end of chapter 41, the challenge was complete. Job had demanded from God the right to order his life. But when God showed up, Job realized his folly. First he acknowledged God's sovereignty, the fact that God is completely in control:

> Job answered the LORD and said, "I know that You can do all things, and that no purpose of Yours can be thwarted."
>
> (v. 42:1–2)

Humbled and ashamed, Job also admitted his foolishness in questioning God's wisdom.

> I have declared that which I did not understand, things too wonderful for

*me, which I did not know ... Therefore I
retract, and I repent in dust and ashes.*

(v. 42:3, 6)

Fear-of-the-Lord Faith

Job had come full circle, finally returning to the
silent, trusting acceptance of chapters 1–2. Hand
over his mouth, Job withdrew all his accusations
of mismanagement against God. He withdrew
all his complaints and stopped all his angry
"Why?" questions. Was it because God gave
Job the answers he had demanded? No. Was it
because God explained how Job's calamity would
eventually lead to good—something good enough
to make it all worth it? No. Was it because God
removed his calamity? No.

When Job saw God's sovereign authority and
infinite wisdom as revealed in creation, Job
realized that explanations weren't necessary. If
God knew why things had happened, Job didn't
need to. God had a plan, and Job wasn't going to
produce a better one. Instead of trying to find
peace in explanations and negotiations, Job lost
himself in a Person—One so wise and so great that
Job could trust him whether Job understood his
painful trials or not.

Childlike faith means that children don't demand that their dad pull over so they can examine the map when the family is driving to Grandma's house. Even if they don't know the way, they trust their father to get them there. Isn't that how Job responded after he met God? He went from demanding the map to being content to rest peacefully in the hands of the Mapmaker.

To order the lives of his human creatures, God instantaneously and constantly assembles, disassembles, and reassembles a six-billion-piece jigsaw puzzle once every second, fitting together the events of the lives of every person on earth to form a perfect picture called his will. As a pebble causes ripples in a pond, so every event in your life causes little waves to wash up on the shores of the lives of the people around you. Change one event in your life, and God's plan for someone two continents away will somehow be affected. The complexity of it is dizzying; only God can plan and administrate it.

Job's enflamed soul was soothed by his tour of creation. God was right. Job couldn't oversee or manage the easy thing (the creation); how could he arrange people's lives? Job was so impressed by the infinite wisdom of the Creator God that he could only respond to God with awe, faith, trust, and submission—the fear of the Lord.

CONCLUSION

For thirty chapters, Job threw all the toys out of his playpen, demanding that God explain what was going on. Did all that pleading, demanding, and arguing help him? No. What helped Job was a fear-of-the-Lord faith. What helped Job was a calm, conscious choice to trust God no matter how great the pain. Job with his hand over his mouth in chapter 40 is a much more relaxed, peaceful, God-honoring Job than the sputtering, fuming Job of chapters 3–31. Imitate Job in chapter 40 (and in chapters 1–2), not in chapters 3–31.

Job's losses were restored many times over (v. 42:10–17), but that wasn't the key to Job's change of heart. The key to his change of heart was the fact that God gave Job himself. In God, Job found answer enough for all his questions.

God won't visit you in a tornado as he did Job, but he doesn't have to: he gave you the book of Job to read. More than that, God has already visited us in his Son, Jesus Christ. The book of Job explains or highlights God's sovereignty, wisdom, and goodness in marvelous ways; Jesus does so even better. According to John 1:1 he is the Word—God's greatest Sermon. In fact, to know God the Son is to know the Father's glorious divine essence. The night before his crucifixion Jesus proclaimed to his disciples,

> He who has seen Me has seen the Father.
> (John 14:9)

Later that same evening, Jesus prayed,

> This is eternal life, that they may know You, the only true God, and Jesus Christ whom You have sent.
> (John 17:3)

Today God has given us himself in Jesus Christ. Through faith in Jesus's death on the cross and his glorious resurrection, we are saved from the greatest calamity ever: hell. Trusting God for forgiveness through Christ brings eternal peace with God in place of judgment (Romans 5:1). And, ultimately, that peace is the basis for all the peace, comfort, and strength God gives to negotiate trials.

In short, a Job-like faith today starts with faith in Jesus Christ.

To sum up, the book of Job warns you not to torture yourself by trying to argue with, negotiate with, or demand answers from God. It warns you of the hazards of listening to well-intentioned but unbiblical counsel. It warns against the trap of time, the snare of expectations, and the danger of lowering the shield of faith. But the primary lessons of the book of Job are about God himself. God is in control—never doubt it. God is wise—trust him. God is good—you can rest in him, even if you don't understand what he is doing.

Leave the planning and ordering of your life and the lives of those you love to God—the God who is all-wise and completely in control. That fear-of-the-Lord faith—an awed, humble, accepting, trusting faith founded on Jesus Christ—is what you need to handle your calamities. Suffering isn't easy; at times you will long for answers to your questions. But when you meet the God of Job 38–41, you find that *he* is answer enough.

Personal Application Projects

1. What expectations have you had that have been disappointed by a calamity that you or someone else has experienced? List them and pray for God's grace to humbly accept his sovereign overruling of your plans.

2. As comfort, joyfully consider what the following verses say about God's shepherding care for his people: John 10:11–15, 27–30; Psalm 23; Isaiah 40:10–11.

3. Read Isaiah 40 and see how many attributes of God you can pick out. How does each attribute contribute to God's ability to care for those going through calamity?

4. When Christians face calamities, they need to be good historians, remembering God's gracious work in the past (Psalm 22:4–5). List ten ways in which God has been good to you in the past, and thank him for each.

5. To help you trust God, review the following
    verses about God's wisdom, sovereignty, and
    shepherding goodness: Psalm 3:3; 4:8; 27:1;
    34:8, 17, 19; 68:19; 119:50, 68, 71, 165; 139:1–24;
    145:14.

6. Four keys to handling calamity include
    thankful prayer, comforting others,
    confidence that God hears our prayers,
    and faithful church attendance. Consider
    what the following verses say on those
    subjects: Philippians 4:6–7; Psalm 34:15; 116:1;
    2 Corinthians 1:3–4; Hebrews 10:24–25.

Where Can I Get More Help?

Adams, Jay E., *How To Handle Trouble God's Way* (Phillipsburg, NJ: P&R, 1982)

Bridges, Jerry, *Trusting God: Even When Life Hurts* (Colorado Springs, CO: NavPress, 1990)

Carson, D. A., *How Long, O Lord? Reflections on Suffering and Evil* (Nottingham: InterVarsity Press, 2006)

James, Joel, *Taste and See That the Lord Is Good: A Study of the Attributes of God* (Leominster: Day One, 2011)

BOOKS IN THE HELP! SERIES INCLUDE...

More titles in preparation

For current listing go to: www.shepherdpress.com/lifeline

About Shepherd Press Publications

» They are gospel driven.

» They are heart focused.

» They are life changing.

Our Invitation to You

We passionately believe that what we are pub-
lishing can be of benefit to you, your family,
your friends, and your work colleagues. So we
are inviting you to join our online mailing list so
that we may reach out to you with news about
our latest and forthcoming publications, and with
special offers.

Visit:

www.shepherdpress.com/newsletter
and provide your name and email address.